Contents

Keening:

Keening

with

Spittal Tongues

Poems

Kathleen Kenny

These poems are dedicated to the memory of my mam, Teresa, her sister, Nellie, and all the clanswomen of Rafferty's Close, in the parish of Kilcoo, Newcastle County Down.

Apologia

To all those women

the ones you imagine
in muddied petticoats
and full grey dresses,

apple-cheeked
and hot-tempered,
running shoeless

in myths of redness.

To all those women

in myths of redness,
their flame-shot hair,
chasing the air

running like me
from being made
by others.

Cover painting: *The Well* by Pauline Kenny
Cover design: Leah Page

Spittal Tongues:

Those Glorious Julys

Teresa has Ulster stamped through her
like Newcastle rock.

July tenth 1915, screaming her entry
and within two days sensing

that she'd learn soon enough
how to keep her mouth shut

for as long as she breathed
in this region of Down.

And when she should leave,
even then, discretion,

the advice:
avoid July.

Mourna's Reel

For the promise of white lace necks
on ringleted daughters
you will all leap off
across the water,

spend eternities on dancing frocks,
embroidering the Celtic cross
for all your frisky-kneed girls:
the new English champions of Ireland.

And I am here still,
stepping the centuries on Ulster stone
with no hard shoes to save me,
disconnect me from the Irish sod.

*Mourna Ban Rua represents the red-headed woman of Irish myth.

Newcastle upon Tyne
1950s/60s

Kathleen Mavourneen
in the Key of Tyneside

At her singing knees
I hear tunes of the past,
the talk of water,
the long trek over:
learn nothing
of my mother's life
except stories.

Offspring

I am making a clearing
learning how to tell
when everything is dark,
green from green from green.

Not South Shields, Whitley Bay, Cullercoats or Tynemouth

Dundrum Bay,
I always knew it:
its pull
its heartbeat
under the grass
its thunder
close as
the Mournes
falling waters
its nearing
as she took
for the day
Uncle William's cart
all the way
from Ballygorian
to the great
open bay
at Newcastle.

Ulster on Tyne

Every St Patrick's Day it arrives:
Auntie Nellie's box of shamrock.

We leave for Mass decked out,
our luscious chests bushy with cress.

Today we're as Irish as our mam's stew

and as with the Ashes that bring in Lent,
identifiably Catholic.

Through our green door, marked out
we fall into Elswick.

Catty cats, English kids bat.
Proddy dogs, we lob back.

Mission

Behind our emerald door
fingers dip, touch the sludge
that lines the well of Holy Water.

We bless ourselves, genuflect;
sisters playing nuns, reliving the shock:
Audrey Hepburn's hair hacked off,

her poor-lovely locks, lost for the love of God
in *The Nun's Story*. A film at last
that made mam happy. Audrey was a vision,

maybe she will grace the Vocations' Exhibition
when it visits Newcastle's Town Moor,
brings with it multitudes of joyous Religious.

Each Holy Order distinctive,
so many stalls it's hard to decide;
more callings than the Hoppings has rides.

Should I be a Franciscan Missionary
or a Sister of Mercy,
a Good Shepherd or a Poor Clare?

Our Pauline would rather be a priest,
but without the veil, I don't see the appeal.
Something blue for me, floaty, semi-transparent,

not heavy, not black. Maybe I'll go somewhere hot
and wear white. I wrap myself in a sheet,
rosary beads at my belt.

When I take the veil
I might call myself Mother Bridget,
our mam's name in the convent.

Unlike her I will not turn back.
I will fulfil the ambition,
an Irish tradition: each generation

donating at least one priest or nun.
I will progress
beyond postulant and novice.

I will marry God, be professed,
unless my hair grows very long,
becomes just too gorgeous to chop.

The Curiosity

Once a fortnight Auntie Nellie writes,
keeps mam's sights on County Down gossip.

Over to visit, she tracks us round town,
up and down Clayton Street
'til her legs inflate like tyres.
At the snack bar in Woolworths
the adults scoff scones and cake,
communicate closely face to face

while we suck Pepsi,
chew fat ham rolls,
mouth to Embassy Record clones:
The Twist with Rikki Henderson,
Bobby Stevens, Paul Rich.

Nellie's shopping bags are filled:
silk ties for the men, and for herself
a hat with a net the colour of buttermilk.
Our mam approves her sister's new clothes,
the matching set:
daffodil dress, daffodil shoes, daffodil coat.

When they laugh they look alike,
reflect each other's source of life,
though Nellie is bigger.

From now on I will picture her,
will hear her lilt exact in my head
as I filch those letters
have every word read and re-read,
stored: water to well.

Protected Species

Auntie Nellie fears for him,
thinks him fragile as new skin,
thin shell.
We watch her
buttering his bread
sugaring his tea
shaving his chin.

Forbidden to complain
we watch him
drumming our cutlery
on our furniture, our crockery,
incessantly
switching over the TV
heedless of us.

That's Leonard
Auntie Nellie smiles.
That's Leonard
our mother sighs.
That's Leonard
they unify
when he wanders off

up to Holy Island,
Seahouses, The Farnes.
Landing back
late at night,
the fate of four eggs
bluebell fine and delicate,
held in his hands.

Another Martyr for Auld Ireland

Another Murder for the Crown

When she comes over this time
Auntie Nellie brings Cousin John:
the young ginger one,
cute though because of the twang.

God love him, she says all the time
and after a while our mam joins in,
is back to talking just like them:
God rest her; Bless us and save us;

Heaven be praised.
For weeks after they go back
she's at the front window
gazing out over our street

as if it's Newcastle County Down
not Newcastle upon Tyne,
like an isolated rebel under attack
singing *Kevin Barry* to keep sane.

Newcastle County Down
1960s

The Returning

Maggie, not as I pictured her,
but frail, in loose black linen,
old and white and wizened,
stepping to the light

from the thick-walled cottage,
giving long lost greetings
to her nieces returning,
great nieces never met.

I look at her face, smiling
and my mother's and my aunts'.
They have sunshine hats, cream-cake grins,
flowered frocks with electric linings.

They chatter about boats, crossings,
the Larne to Belfast train,
the landlady, the boarding house,
Newcastle, and how it's changed.

They pass pink rose cups,
discuss the taste of scone;
how Uncle Michael's getting on
as he potters in and out looking lost.

Mam is spreading butter:
oh the wonder of Maggie's bread,
the hospitable hag has us so well fed
we are fit to bursting.

Full of home-made baking
and second-hand spite
I contemplate Maggie:
the object of my mother's hate,

wonder about the childhood damage
she still carries like a crate.
All the while
more plates are passed:

harvest cake crusted with sugar,
suffused with bitter purple plum.

Beanna Bóirche

I am on my back
listening to the earth,
the water throwing itself
down the length of the Mournes,

the mountains whispering
the past:
St Donard saying Mass;
tales and legends,

the claim of names and flags,
while under me
green and orange intertwine, unite,
and I lie scraped and veined and mottled,

my purple-heathered knees
sticking up and out from me
like Slieve Donard and Slieve Thomas,
falling open under the black sky.

* Beanna Bóirche was the Gaelic name for the Mountains of Mourne,
  still being used in the seventeenth century.

The Accident

Hardy as the rain-soaked fields,
Uncle Mick leans on his spade,
to rest his back,
pushes back his worn-out hat,
takes the wet from his forehead
with the cuff of his jacket.

He's ninety-two and wiry as a fence.
Tonight as always
he will take the bike from the shed,
clip back the wide legs
of his Sunday trousers
and peddle to Lizzie Greenan's.

After seeing off a pint,
he will hail his goodnights,
will crunch the red and black bike
through the pebbles of the car park,
before fluttering off like a kite,
a ribbon

midnight blue and singing,
not seeing the last Hilltown bus,
not hearing the fuss
as he is thrown under.

As he bites the dust,

back in the pub, the regulars will discuss
the benefits of work, of keeping fit in old age.
Then they will raise their glasses, toast:
Years from now let's hope that's us.
Long live Mick.

Newcastle County Down
1920s

Black and Tans

Open in the King's name, they shout.
Doesn't that man have a lot to answer for?
Their grandmother, from the cottage, gives out.

At her knee Nellie and Teresa quake.
A felled tree blocks the foot of the Close
but nothing bars their way: least of all bravado.

The orphans and the old woman wait
soon they will hear dark boots retrace the hill,
Rafferty's lane will once again fall still,

leaving them free to clear away the tree,
strip it of leaves and twigs.
When the men come in from hiding

they will mark it, saw it into logs:
wood always comes in handy
for heating water, warming clothes,

and in the hopeful work of sabotage.

Troubles

Every stick in the house
is moved out.

Taking tea in the yard,
their grandmother is cursing:
They're going to burn us out.

As the heavens open up
on all they have.

Irish Linen

From the beginning
visible by his absence,
missing the linen fields

in their feast of blue pastel.
If you had the day
you could spend it

staring by the edge,
watch it being pulled up by the roots
where the flax was.

Before being spread on the bleach greens
it was soaked in troughs
dug out by the road.

On hot days Nellie and Teresa
pulled off their stockings,
plodged the unspun cloth;

never needed to worry
about their father
turning up to tell them off.

Maggie's Story

New Woman of the House

I can hardly refuse:
the cottage, as well as the fields.
And though he's twice my age,
he keeps the faith, is presentable enough.

As for the parasites: those sulky girls;
his brothers and their appetites,
I'll see them cleared out,
those that are able,

and those that aren't must learn,
things will be different.
Lord knows, my husband
will be on my bones soon enough,

raising the roof with his moans.
Please God I will teach him to be quiet.
Decorum, I'll have it:
my compensation.

And Praise Be
there'll be children of our own.
Our own mouths to feed. New priorities.
Michael will come to see it soon enough.

Teresa's Story

Summer Nights

Let's settle for
a summer's dusk, say 1924,
me and Nellie racing the lane,
reaching the Square exhausted.

Some of our cousins already there,
a gathering of Sunday-scrubbed youth.
Testing new jokes we lean back,
laugh into the mellow sun,
keep our tongues wet and warm and busy.

Father McKenna on his, *coincidental*
walk back to the presbytery,
is slippery, dusts over us
his evening eyes.

This is all we have,
no dance hall or radio,
but the Crossroads,
some music, a storyteller perhaps.
What passes for amusement, what passed.

Separation

in memory of Peggy and Bob

I've learned to rise at first light,
fetch water from the well,
get breakfast for the pigs and hens,

collect eggs, milk cows, muck out.
I've learned to lift potatoes,
sidestepping dirt the digger spits out

as I follow it up the field.
I know how to churn butter from sour milk,
strain it, salt it lightly, pat it into shape.

Up in Belfast, my far off uncles and aunts
raise my brother and sister as strangers,
at a removal of thirty miles odd.

I'm told they keep a cat with fur to the mat;
that they buy from a store with three separate floors,
and take their water from a tap.

When I visit I will see street lamps
dimming the night sky,
I will learn about things like distance and belonging.

Driving the Cows

By the rump of the last cow
my red waves bob and blow and bow.
Over thick steamy hide
I wave my bony stick,
am running and running,
running the cows.

Hurry now, shouts Uncle Mick,
The sooner to market, the sooner you're rich.
My plate-white bones itch,
tonight they will ache, click-clack complaint,
as blood fattens me, reddens my face
with the heat of work and a good scrub.

Before bed, the private pleasure of my head,
I will be fed, smiled at perhaps,
then when I lift my swift-cleaned plate
my eyes will light
lick, taste:
ten great shillings.

The Haggle

A pair of black leaden lace-ups
stare sombrely out from O'Neill's shop front.
They are slack at the heels, but Uncle Michael feels
my feet will fit them perfectly inside a fortnight.

He can practically see them growing he says to me,
and then to Mr. O'Neill before the chance of any choice:
For pity's sake, the child's an orphan,
could you not see your way to moving down the price?

Feeling Bravely

When he's got the drink
I play him up,
his pity for my state
makes him generous but

when he's got the drink
Uncle Thomas is full of threats:
what he won't do to my dad
if he ever gets the chance.

On such nights I don't rest.
What if he finds that rogue Ned,
comes staggering back
bragging of his murder?

I'd rather have a shilling
instead of Ned's blood.
I'd rather have a shilling
from a clean pair of hands,

hear Uncle Thomas land,
not measuring the lane this time
but stepping a straight line.
Feeling bravely: just a little delicate.

Not Dipping the Sheep

I slip away

leave the long day by the fence,
fall into dry summer grass, press
my face through the skin of the pond.

It laps my tongue, takes the heat.
Uncle Mick and Smart are beat,
look towards the sound of water,

wonder where I went.

Simple

While we're out collecting the flour
my new aunt Maggie puts his bed
into the byre, says there's insufficient space,
from now on he must sleep with the cows.

Tomorrow I will fly to Uncle William's,
relate his brother's plight,
he will put it right, get the police
to see the bed brought back into the house.

When they call, Uncle Peter will not be about,
he'll be in the top field, out of earshot,
out of sight: shouting to the mountains
all the bad words he knows

fit to describe her.

The Turnip Eaters

Our faces are white powder
as we bump the sack of flour all the way
back up Rafferty's Close on the barrow.

Uncle Peter has had enough
of picking turnip muck from his teeth,
feeding himself on their sweet raw yellow.

If she's agreeable, he says,
we'll have wheaten bread tomorrow.
If she's agreeable

we'll have cooked dinner
instead of scrapings from the field,
we'll lick away our plates,

clean our tongues of dirt.
We'll have a rare day indeed,
if she's agreeable.

Blood, Land and Adolescence

Whenever I get the chance I escape, take
the Upper Road to Uncle William's farm of land.
He and Mary Ann are childless,
have promised me all this if I stay.

But haven't I seen enough of working this land
and am I not pleased to be skipping
like a mountain goat
all three fields off the road,

chased down to their cottage
by the McIllvenny lads,
their hot mouths calling after me
until we're all breathless?

My small forgetfulness stretches
to such a ballyhoo and fuss
for just a few gates left unshut
and a mix-up of livestock that strayed.

I want no farm of land, I say.
I wouldn't stay, and I won't.

Uncle William the Taleteller

Most of them I knew were made up,
but the one about his dead boyhood friend
was real enough.

The ghost of young Ted catching him up
on the road, the very road
they'd strode together as boys.

In the name of God, is it you? William cried.
It was true. Ted required a Mass or two
for the repose of his soul: hitherto neglected.

At sunrise, William, still petrified, paid the price
of four Masses to the big eyes of Father Fitzpatrick
and was thereafter left in peace.

As always when he finished a story,
he leaned forward, scratched his bottom lip,
ended with: *Stick that in your pipe and smoke it.*

Woman of the Roads

She caught me at the Crossroads
on my way back to Rafferty's Close.

Don't be going there, she warned,
that place is full of prig women.

Luckily I've been taught not to listen,
know all about dirt and sinning,

women like her tramping the roads,
claiming to see what's hidden,

clinging to the basket
she never puts down, never lets go.

But I know what's in it:
a dead baby,

or a wee divil
she lets out at night to do her bidding.

Mourna Ban Rua, mad old crone.
As if she can see what's hidden,

as if there's a choice about where to go.

The Spinsters

When they pass on,
the tradition of a white plume
will adorn the undertaker's hat,
mark their single status,
their innocence in the ways of the flesh.

The Parish of Kilcoo will be less for their going
but will remember their kindnesses,
how they just couldn't bear it:
a small child, practically without a stitch,
every cold school day, sliding past
the width of their warm cottage.

That one winter's gift
which carries itself in my head,
growing as I fill out
their hand-stitched coat;
making me think I will come back

chosen as a nun perhaps,
to tell them of my vocation,
my unblemished life
of prayer and purity
which one day might afford me too
the privilege of a white plume.

The Convent
1930s

Fast Food

Each Friday two of us walk
from Brockley Rise to Honor Oak
take the train to London Bridge
to buy fresh fish from Billingsgate
to feed the sisters.

Away from the confines
of the convent my black-toed boots
shine with relief, dance my feet
like feathers until we leave,
heaving back the fruits of the sea.

Sauntering through the trays of fish
my heart sings to a Latin beat,
my taste develops a passion
in later life for sole, and plaice,
and an attachment to Civvy Street.

IRA Dreams in the Sacred Heart

Every day at six I make
my way to sing in chapel,
though mostly we serve
under rule of silence,
thirty-six women living in peace.

Sister Eugene is a chatter-box
always in hot water
for disobeying the short hours
of recreation
when we are allowed to speak;

the rest of the time
restricted to whispers,
and only on matters of work,
meals are taken silently
listening to the Lord's Word.

At nine we retire to our cells
where no utterance is dared,
heaven help the sleep-talkers
Mother Superior
will have your head.

Sister Eugene dreads the dark:
those visits from her parents
murdered in their beds,
all that they might say to her,
and what she might impart.

The Miracle of Lourdes

towards Italy

Divining the future,
her knees numb in mud,
her fingers scraping soil, digging,
then it comes, a dribble at first,
tears seasoning the tongue
with sprigs of salt.

The Lady smiles on, until it's done.
A surge of joy for the little one, scruffy
and scuffed. Oh Lord, what she has spawned:
a Holy Spring where we will flood to be cured;
where we will leave our cloaks and dip like salmon
 praying to be pink and clean and healthy.

This town full of relics, priests and nuns,
plastic bottle-tops like blue crowns,
screw them off and dip your fingers
into transparent liquid skulls.
This is what's to come
of her little piece of living,

her life of sacrifice and visions,
endeavouring to be good and pure,
a devout, obedient nun.
Bernadette, martyr to the grotto,
her sainthood assured. My train moves on.

Approaching the New Convent

Urns lining the platform,
sparks of sun: nineteen-thirty-five
on the Mediterranean.
All is blue as I step off the train
at Stazione Ospedaletti.
This is me, a Cabrini Sister
asking Cabinerri for directions.

*

In the next century
imagine I have a daughter
who follows me, to find
the beaten out carriage
of a rusted past,
an endless pebble path
where the line once was.

From the Shade
of a Straw Hat

Behind the black-feathered tree
the sky is lemon,
there is a sheen of brown velvet
on the roots of the nun-house.

From the outside
it's like a touched-up postcard
trying to be appreciated
for its delicacy of shadow and light.

Like those pictures of old Ireland
where the green is greenest,
and the blue is bluest,
and the whitewash shows no reason

for you to travel to this convent,
in this season on the continent,
behind the black-feathered trees
in Italy where the sky is lemon.

Mother Bridget

When I took my new name I hoped
to become a nurse for one of the Order's
convents in Africa, or America,
never saw myself as a teacher, or here

leaning on a fig tree in this rich orchard,
squinting from a panama,
my citrus tongue shiny with acceptance:
vows of obedience.

Before meals we all
must stand for Mussolini,
except for me and Sister Eugene
who, as Irish, are exempted.

The bay of Dundrum
so cold and far away now,
and the light from the old cottage,
a distant speck on a dark mountain.

The Line to Ospedaletti

Picture this disused,
all spinning off
into a tunnel of thistle
no break in the fence,
the coastal path
becoming cliff
no left or right turn
only the long lost railroad,
the straight miles ahead,
the ears doubt about
that distant thrum,
the rattle of metal:
metal wheels on metal.

Newcastle County Down
1990s

The Keening

I'll Take You Home Again Kathleen

Black shoreline. The Mournes
fixed against a deep-set wind.
Faces filled with generations,
collective wills:
fetching water,
bending,
birthing,
digging the earth
always
heading out away from
or heading back towards
the bay.

Trip

Jimmy McAvoy spots
cousin Leonard at the bus stop
taps his small haversack,
asks: *Is it a day trip to Belfast?*
No, says Leonard,
it's three weeks in Africa.

On Nellie's Death

In Teresa's stead
me and Pauline: her youngest,
carry last respects
back to her sister in Ireland.

On the plane we share out thoughts:
our last trip over
taxiing Nellie up to Bryansford,
laying daisies on Herbie, her son,

a linking-chain she will now join.
Near right of the front gate
the two old graves marked
in stone: Green and Rafferty,

our Shimna vein, covered
uncovered, hot muscle
on the digger's shovel, blood
on bone, on bone.

Cousins

Engulfed by rooftop smoke
blown down in the wind
we knock, cough, wait,
hinged between broken glass
and a slice of winter jungle.

The door slowly opens.
From low half-spectacles
Leonard explores the dark,
our faces.

His jaw drops, apologizes:
Cousins, step in,
I thought for a moment
you were someone come
to offer condolences.

Sons

John returns from Canada
the day after his mother's death.

Leonard, bird-watching in Africa,
jets back on the eve of the funeral.

When we arrive: the female side,
John is on the phone:

Micháel wants to know
if you will view the remains?
Leonard breaks from his crossword,
deliberates: *Aye,* he says, *aye, I will.*

It's arranged, one last exchange
half an hour before the Requiem.

Family Notice

The notice in the *Irish Times,*
only three sons mentioned:
Leonard and John still living,
Herbie passed on.

                    Gerry absent.

Gerard is difficult,
a surname not his brothers'
but his mother's maiden name,
this amounts to printing the word

                    Bastard.

Also, Gerry disappeared.
Is he late then
or just missing?
After all this time,
the past again

                    keeping John awake.

The wake: one more sleepless night.
Before heading out he makes a call
to correct the omission:

   Gerard, Herbert, Leonard, John.

Gerard

We recall you that spring, gardening on Woodside
in shirt-sleeves, in apple blossom.
And before, staying with us one summer;
vanishing behind the stained-glass door
with a single spoon and a massive block of Wall's,
eating it all, locked in alone. Licking the cardboard clean.

Later we heard our mother talk of brilliance,
a thesis you wrote,
the thin line between madness and genius.
But we were interested more by your eye:
lost on a bacon slicer
while working as a youngster in a grocery store.

We wondered what secrets you kept under the patch
though never asked you to lift it up.
The unspeakable more fascinating by far, than your feats:
winning a cup, being the fastest boy up Slieve Donard.
Only the dark stuff intrigued us: your stay in York Asylum,
the dispute over land, money buried in muck, disappearance.

The caravan deserted, left as if you'd just popped out for milk.
Speculation ran about the deed, its nature and motives.
Was it suicide, terrorists, money, murder, greed?
Were you dumped in a lime-pit, or did you just emigrate?
Which ever it was you left no trace: police, press,
Salvation Army, even the clairvoyant who went against

the priest, couldn't turn you up.
After seven years you were declared dead
but kept warm by Nellie's hope:
here she always held as right the last sighting of you that night
speeding out of Newcastle on a motorbike,
heading south towards the border.

Herbert

Two weeks from the altar
young Herbie was jilted:
found dead on an English street.
In between lies
the matter of time,
the matter of drink.

The Sawyers: cousins, who have
the undertakers; the bookies;
the taxies; and two sons priests,
brought him home cheap
over water, laid him at Bryansford
where a small rose bowl marks him.

Immediately underneath is Ned,
not marked, but present.
A drunk. He beat his family,
deserted his first young. Now
under death, he is back: glue
wedging what remains, weighty bones.

Between us we piece bits of them
together, weave half-histories
passed on from our mothers,
what they seemed to believe:
one man's naivety and goodness,
the purposeful evil of the other.

The Grave Crasher

We remember the stink:
the call on Nellie's charity.
Ned's second family, without money
and with no family plot.

The priest's plea
for a space in the Rafferty grave:
He's nowhere else to go,
he begged, *and* you*'re all he's got.*

Songs

John began a song,
told us how he found his voice
crossing the Atlantic.

His brother Leonard
never left County Down but sings
in karaokes at the Donard:

Mack the Knife
with his hat on a slant,
jaunty, just like Sinatra.

Clear Out

Will they fit Auntie Teresa?
John wonders, bringing through
a pair of Nellie's sandals,
and the new slippers, still stiff,
sticking out from the tapestry bag
that smells of Meppo and coins and candles.
At the bottom some medals
are threaded through with blue fleck.
One is Miraculous.

And here is her pitted-leather missal,
its places kept with gold, and white ribbons,
holy pictures, cards: *In memoriam,* treasured.
One commemorates Maggie,
the woman my mother calls the auld bitch,
who married their Uncle Mick
and took over the cottage
when their grandmother died.

I touch her prayers, her blessings,
her likeness. She is old in this,
smiling, innocuous;
making me wonder why it is
that Auntie Nellie chose to keep her precious,
why it is that John
thinks sisters' feet should match,
should fit each other's slippers?

Keening

The old rite denounced, though not passed away,
here tonight it is cast in the form of a rosary.
The women of the parish keen the newly dead.

With chants they lift Nellie from the coffin-bed,
dance her overhead on an air of blue incense,
in a gold jig of candle-flame, on moaning tongues.

Here tonight at the Receiving In,
they are making rhythm, a cradling-frame.
They are humming her life, saying her.

*Keening: a chant for the dead, denounced by the Roman Catholic Church.

Burial

Nellie's second son waits,
soon her remains
will be placed on his.

For now she rubs against
her living sons, turning
their necks red, upsetting
the lie of Leonard's bright tie.

Her boys: pallbearers, bitten
by winter and grief, process
through the streets to Bryansford.

On Dundrum Bay the Mournes
play their mystery, clasp shadows
to arms, Leonard and John
clinging on under the weight.

At the grave ropes slip into place.
The men tender: loosening,
lowering, touching.

Malaria

I don't feel the cold. Leonard says,
twelve hours after
his return from Africa.

Burying his mother
his thin jacket shudders,
someone walking his grave.

Serengeti mud splatters
the hem of his beige trousers
hanging half-mast over DM's.

Boy-man, sea-blue and clear,
deep as a well-used grave.
He knows every bird

on the east Ulster coastline,
and is the first man from Newcastle
to reach the final of 15 to 1.

The Donard

From outside, we admire
domes of red brick,
edges and tips
worked in black slate
to look like gothic towers.

Over a pint John explains
the skill of our grandfather:
how Ned's craft helped build this place,
create its arches and points,
its intricacies.

Next day we drive out from Newcastle,
take in complex patterns in Hilltown,
Tollymore, down in Castlewellan.
Ned could make anything happen
with brick, or clay, or stone.

Up in Kilcoo, while working
on the church of St Malachy
he met, wooed and won
the young Mary Rafferty,
pledged her his craftsmanship,

his hands, something of value:
the ability to earn enough
to raise a family,
drink the Donard dry.

Rebel

John wants to join in
but worries about the lyrics

being too Republican. Somewhere
outside there is growling

but in here everyone knows
the words.

Beginning and End

The day before we leave
John drives us out, past
Tollymore, through Bryansford
by the graves,
on and up to Rafferty's place.

At the cottage we let
ourselves through the gate,
straight to the back fence
where the fields start.
We lift the outhouse latch
see the well,
our family drawing water.

All the dead
stepping down to drink
and the spring-bathed face
of Mourna Ban Rua,
just like in the picture.

Take Off

At Belfast Harbour we settle in,
boiled sweets and gin all the way to England.
For days we have been keeping him
from leaving the ground, but now
after dropping us, John is off
to sing in his cups down at the Donard.

After lock-in he snakes to the take-out,
rolls down to the bay, to find again
the cloud like Nellie's hair, the sand
that glints a smile, invites him to jump
down awhile, curl in its grain.

Tomorrow, fragile, flying back to Canada
John will blame jet-lag,
will rack his brain without success,
to explain the ear cut clean across,
the tear in his head:
the great thickness of lost blood.

Mourna and the Well

I spring from the land
of the Mournes
where the red-headed women dwell,
I live in the breath
of Rafferty's cottage,
in the water drawn up from the well.

I fill the pail that Nellie carries,
I spill and I wash and I swell.
Over the fire I sting,
deliver the stew
that is served to the men.

Michael, William, Peter, Thomas,
and all the rest
bending their heads
at the watery steps
their bubbled knees, strong necks,
swirls of laughter, breath on stone.

Newcastle upon Tyne
2000s

Homesick

Garvaghy Road, Drumcree.
Isn't it everything I know, Teresa says.

Isn't it a great place
to be away from.

Those Glorious Skies

On its eleven-hundredth-and-forty-fifth trip
around her, the next full moon

will pull Teresa up,
move her to switch off the big light,

inch across the silver sitting room
to her window above the motorway.

Glorious, she will say, looking up,
knowing that what she sees above

is a dim version of her childhood vision
from the Mournes;

that city nightscapes fog things
with their squints of orangegreen artificial light,

clogging our blood so we forget
how to read this map of dark delights,

and all our grandmothers said
about the behaviour of the Heavens:

the stars, birds, colours and clouds,
all we need to know about tomorrow,

sought in the nature of sky.

Spittal Tongues

Avoiding Study
in the History Annexe

Newcastle University

Pressed 1471, pressed 3, tried Telewest,
thought about Ponteland, flooded:
standing on the bridge of the River Pont,
walking through the Black Gate
during the plagues,
the Civil War, the Restoration.

Listened to Marianne, sang,
mused about mulled wine,
Rachael and Leah at the Labour Club.
In my office opposite Claremont car park
I thought about my watch, raindrops,
twinkling eyes, and glistening anoraks,

the way ash glows on cigarettes:
talking earlier to Jenny
in Fenwicks' crockery shop
about her joining Brian in Florida.
(They are finally out, after all
the cloak and dagger stuff.)

The radiator in here is red hot,
it saves money being away from the house.
When this MA is done I'll be on my own,
moving on from the family home,
and this, my city-centre bolthole:
its safe escapes and pleasures.

Housebound with Flowers

One-five-seven-one:
two messages from mam.

One saying she's going out now,
and won't be back
for the rest of the evening.

The other being grateful:
thanking me
for the chrysanthemums

some other daughter sent.

Old Age is a Pig

The tongue of a hungry cat
licks the cold meat of your brain,
cleans the inside of your skull

until you unlearn something every day.
How many candles
on this cake of black molasses?

You slacken your grip,
struggle to live,
pick at dirt, black pith, grime.

What food is this:
chicken neck; tuna slime;
horse-meat in jelly?

The crusted belly, its final swelling.
The burned fat of that pig
dripping though time.

New Leafs

We don't accept it yet
but one of us is near death,
one of us set on making
an exhibition of herself,
leaving home, for life,
looking to be adventurous

while there's still time:
some hormones stirring.

But I don't want to be found
by you, in a flat, without
husband or house. The knot
of that failure crumples me
as I peer over our Moor:
see all that was, what has to be,

leaves turning,
swirling through our history.

Blue Day with Chopped Hair

I polish my steamy spectacles
flatten my kiss-curl,
make my way up the stairs
weighted with library books.

This late education designed
to fill the void of grown children,
this uni room, a godsend
I am turning into a surrogate home

where I store my guilt,
lightweight, placed next to yours.
You, whose birth was the cause
of your own mother's death.

I have cut my hair, am balanceless,
bereft as a widow,
staring out over the vacant car park,
at a loss to know where I go from here.

Alone and Leathered

After four pints of Scrumpy
in the North Terrace
Brian tells me his room in the Annexe
is haunted by colourful ghosts.

From then on I listen for footsteps
in the passage, look for a spectacle
in scarlet, parrot-green,
kingfisher, maroon, tangerine.

But how am I to know
what sounds ghosts make:
interpret meanings malicious or benign,
intentions vague as men's?

On the way back late that night
silver lights damp my hair, lemonade rain
fizzes off my gabardine, a shandy-black
covering for the ladders I am laced with.

Tin Bath Inheritance

after Frieda Kahlo

A tiny woman on a raft,
ten toes and a tug boat,
volcanoes, skeletons, a plug
swimming towards me,
stopping me going under.

My mother and father
cutting themselves
as they scale the chain,
their blood dripping
into the water.

Rubber ducks, reeds,
rushes, sailing masts,
a damn under construction.
All this debris
and muck. No soap.

My gold taffeta dress
scummy and in ruins.
I am naked, and so
much bigger than anything
I ever imagined.

How Lucky

The thing I didn't know then
when you warned me off
breaking Friday fast,
being late for Mass,
talking to strangers,
bad behaviour: swearing,
cheek, answering back.
The thing I didn't know
when you harped on
the dangers
of going out in this,
catching my death in that,
older men, drinking dens,
walking late alone.
What I didn't know was
when I did come home,
starved and devoured
with an hour to doze
by the newly made fire
before a cat-lick
and back out for work,
you never would remark
on the states I got in
or ask how
my white cat-suit got hacky.
You only cared how I was
brought tea, bread, eggs,
toasties that were just the job.
The things I didn't know,
had no idea of.

All You Could Afford

To me, those beads
were diamonds.
That watch eighteen carat.

Before long
I will thank you for it:
for each and every present.

I will take you on a jaunt,
make that wheelchair your throne,
this aircraft your carriage.

I will toast you in the lounge
of the Slieve Donard.
You will be honoured

with half a beer shandy
and a fit cup of tea.

Taking You Back

It's a hard trip this time:
your love-hate shades of Ulster
have turned pure black, on top
of that the aircraft has lost
your wheelchair. The signs

are set. Nowhere is any good.
The gravel lanes we bump along
drive you bats. The cottage
and the graveyard full of dead clan.
Why would you want to visit them

when even The Good like Uncle William
took you back each time you ran away
from that place you wouldn't grace
with the name of home,
because, like the rest, he only cared

how things looked, and not what you stood
at the hands of the auld-witch-aunt.
Three months Coventry for taking an egg
to ease the hunger. Those soft-boiled Rafferty
men who daren't, even then,
give her the walloping she deserved.

So, as you bring the subject up, and I ask if,
when the time comes,
you would like to see your ashes spread here
on the Mournes, your No is categoric.

Spittal Tongues

the parties

At 2am the night-watch man
shines a torch up to the kitchen.
I wave from the window, go down
and reassure him everything's sound:
I'm working late on an overdue essay.
Upstairs everyone is
smoking, drinking, dancing.
All our voices aloft.

The Annexe of Timid Hearts

The book you kept insisting
you would bring
became a metaphor for promise.

It kept me in your thoughts
until you became so weary
you had to sleep

and dream of this man
with diseased skin,
a painter, exactly like you.

Taking the stairs two by two
you would bring him
to my room: all his images.

We would look at the book,
fingers up sleeves,
your blue chest warming.

You and I together
talk, talk, talking,
all the way to morning:

the dawning of paralysis.

Pointers

Beside your spidery legs
I feel calm,
as if you are befriending me.
Peaceful as a pond on a warm day
I hardly know what to think,
your eyes so amused,
bits of smoke strolling up
your half-closed lids.
I take your hand, squeeze myself
into your baggy sleeve
and sit, watching your shoulders shake,
your nose crease and crinkle
with the effort to control your mirth.
On my new dress drifts of smoke patrol,
work their way overhead
where the morning sun is red:
a shepherd's warning.

Cooking with Rum

Lonely, I give out gifts.
Words and lips arrive
like reciprocal presents.

Hot and momentary
e.g. Steve and Nick:
their soft romantic cakes,

big butter-cream mistakes,
too gungy, not the right
consistency, not the right

something for which I wait.

Purging

You all burn nicely.
I watch your grease
rise from the high chimney,
float in the form of smoke
over the downstairs nursery,
deposit you on the leaves
of the red tree,
in the deceptively large
garden of infancy
where you lived.

Downstairs they take Babies

Subsumed into a pc world
of among other things
working opportunities for women:
the *right* of everyone to work.

I watch them, the working women
wheeling infants into the downstairs
nursery, crowding through the doors
for 8am opening.

One car drops off, another picks up:
the fathers or the minders employed
to look after other women's children
so they too can go out and earn.

Once we were encouraged to pity
Soviet women *forced*
to put their offspring
into crèches and *made to* go to work.

Yet look at this madness down here
in the Annexe yard. Tangles of buggies,
the best buyable baby-mod-cons.
Two used to be the lower limit
but they take them now at six-months.

World Turned Snide

It's hard for those who weren't around
to imagine how it was before the car park,
and the trees planted down there
to disguise the Central Motorway.

I recall when all this land was moor,
before these non-negotiable road dissections.
In historical terms a century is a small thing.
It's not so long since Newcastle hung witches

over there, and men played football without
a care to St James's corporate wealth,
or *security,* and none of our ilk could foresee
the establishment of universities
who suck up fat fees and all creation.

Our self-congratulation makes us fools.
No days of misrule. Young fools today
must be quiet, sly, quick with a knife.
Slip it in. No fracas. No fight.
No enjoyment of a good punch-up.

Admission

A is for angina. *If you have a strong heart how can you suffer?*
B is for blood sample. *If you can't stop bleeding don't blame
me.*

C is for cuff, constriction, concern for her modesty.
D is for dog, one black floating dog: left eye only.
E is for escape, ignore the exit sign, there is none.
F is for the future, finally getting out of this Hospital after a
week-long-day.
G is for groaning, a patient who screams at the squeeze of a
blood pressure band.
H is for history, all the stuff she doesn't remember: her own
medical biography.
I is for I wish I wasn't here, but who else would be?
J is for today's journey, looking through tinted glass, talking
to men in green clothing.
K is for Kathleen, wicked off! (me).
L is for lonely, and Dr Lee, Freeman Casualty.
M is for mercy.
N is for nurses, their busy legs, their pale blue trousers.
O is *for open, say R, let's see your tongue. Put it away.*
P is for *Push me.*
Q is for *quickly.*
R is for running after the wheelchair that skids my mother
backwards to chest x-ray.
S is for sizzled and sizable and someday soon, somehow,
someway.

Legless

Five minutes late for our date
in The Hotspur.
The state of geography
in my own town,
these up-side-down streets,
drizzle on the pavements
like grease. I can't keep my feet,
smash my head going down
and roll, and roll
into the dark wet centre of this road,
where the feet of men pass me by
leave me space to lie paralyzed
without pain though the skin on my face
is ripped, and I can't raise myself
back up, not even to crawl.
Panicking I hear an engine's drawl,
no lights, but the sound of it making forward.
I roll myself from the centre of the lane
to a place where wheels might escape me.
Lucky, but how do I negotiate the thick mud
I'm caked in now, and how do I get up
before more wheels come
and I am crushed into crow food?
What a mess. Why six pints?
Why Scrumpy Jack?
I'm definitely not making it tonight.

New

You seem just right
like the old ted
I ran to pick out
from the pile of toys
in the school hall
when at long-last
my name was called:
a second-hand prize
I wanted to believe
had been made
especially for me,
so much so
we silently agreed
he would
hug no other child
and I would never
replace him.

May Day

for Jeremy

Walking through the quadrangle
after rain. Our heads up

noticing trees in blossom,
the colours of flowers,

the scents of spring.
Newcastle's bright shining sky

over all the emptiness,
and our joined-up fingers.

Disjointed Day

Wet shoes,
the Metro open at the TV page.
Upstairs on the number one
the smell of garlic
and damp students.

A computer warming up.
A kettle cooling down.
Someone jumps a puddle.
At 4-o-clock darkness falls.

The somethings said:

I'm not buying flowers,
not stopping at the shops.
I have crossed
the motorway bridge
and lived.

I am taking the lift
up Hilltop House,
folding a gamp,
listening to my mother
interpreting the weather
from the way the raindrops
hit the glass.

Double Shock

Your mouth fills with blood.
It's yours, you swallow it,
it's thick and black,
neat, but for the tears and spit.

You can't think, can't speak,
there are clots of cotton wool
under the checked scarf
tied tightly round your cheeks.

He has taken out eight teeth.
You still smell the gas,
his rubber mask, the reek of lies:
Only one extraction dear.

You wail all the way home,
disturb everyone on the bus.
She tries to calm you with talk
of tasty slop: home-made broth,
bread and butter pud.

Tomorrow you will stay off school,
she will buy you anything you want:
Brier Rabbit's colouring book
and a whole new set of crayons.

You won't realize there is a time
to come where she is absent from,
a space in your life where she
is gone. So you can't whinge on
about this momentous event from
the past, ever, ever again.

Song

against Colonic Irrigation

All the lush fruits of the earth
I bestow on you. All the figs and dates,
the grapes and orange sunsets,
all spongy-leaves and sleek-coated dogs,
all the greenery and brownery,
the heat and rain, the river boats
and black fertile fields.
I tip all of these on your knees,
squeeze the fires of the sky
between your toes. I bequeath
you my serenity, proclaim you
sovereign of the universe.
Into your hands I place all power,
all might, and helplessness.
I feed all colours into your mouth.
All the smells of the forest
I grease you with.
I touch your neck and legs
and thighs with the sounds of soft water,
tap musical notes out over your eyes
onto your wholesome breakfast
of blueberries and branflakes
and Scotch Porridge Oats.

Brown Eyed Girl
Van Morrison

Seeing this:
your eyes pale,
your eyes paling.

I'll hold on
to your hand
like long ago,

notice the colour
returning:
imagine it, if I must.

Late Blossoming

Today you would be complaining
about the heat
but would still want it,

and to see these blooms:
That plant always waits
for you to water it Kathleen.

Waits for me to home it too,
before it finally flowers.

Now you're free of dotage,
free of the wheelchair, the Zimmer,
waiting for carers to cook your dinner;

free of plants that don't flower until
you've gone to a higher power.

Acknowledgements

Some of these poems were originally published in a pamphlet produced by *Sand Press* (thanks to Kevin Cadwallender, editor). Thanks also to the editors of the following poetry magazines where versions of other poems have appeared: Coffee House, Eclectica, Feile-Festa, First Thought, Hamilton Stone Review, Moodswing, Mousion, Osprey, Poetry Revolt, Pulsar, Revival Poetry Journal, The Tipton Poetry Journal, White Leaf Review.

A special note of thanks goes to Sheila Wakefield, and appreciation as always to friends and fellow writers for their support and encouragement. For advice on *Keening* particular thanks to Brendan Kennelly and Mimi Khalvati. Finally, for their enduring love and support my gratitude goes to Sarah, Leah and Rachael, and also to Jeremy Campbell.